START FROM HERE

DIVYA JAIN

Made with ♥ on the Notion Press Platform
www.notionpress.com

Contents

Acknowledgements

This book is dedicated to the reader who aspires to transform himself. I appreciate God for hearing my unheard prayers and providing me with strength throughout. I'd like to thank my family and teachers for shaping me into the person I am today. My friends, who left no stone unturned in pushing me to achieve my goals and always stood by my side, and my lovely students, who make me smile and shine a little brighter. I'm eternally grateful to everyone who helped me along the way, knowingly or unknowingly. It seemed to be a distant dream until I found Notion Press and got an opportunity to get my first collection of work published.

Introduction

This book is a collection of risk-free, self-tested, self-development strategies.

Since it strives to make you better, this book won't comfort the flawed you.

For folks, who have simply started to read yet find it difficult to finish a book, here is a selection that you can read all the way through. We're all in it together. It will be worth it.

This book is not meant to be devoured in one sitting; rather, proceed slowly and keep in mind the instructions and follow it religiously. Recognize that reading alone won't change anything.

Do not be the kind of person who carries a book everywhere and reads it nowhere.

This book should be placed on your table rather than left to collect dust on the shelf.

If you decide to follow instead of just reading more, there is more room for improvement.

I wish you all the best!

CHAPTER ONE

Power of Tidying up

Okay!

I'm sure you've had experiences when:

- You didn't keep your clothes in order,
- Had a cluttered bookcase,
- A sink full of filthy dishes,
- A shoe rack full of mud and jumbled pairs of shoes,
- Disorganized drawers, and
- A room with no room to live in it.

Now, here's something I'd want to share with you, I've been a messed-up person. I've always had my room, so privacy has always been a part of my life.

In terms of how I used to keep myself, there wasn't much intervention.

I recall getting ready for school and returning home tossing my uniform in various corners of the room, then prepping for coaching, which I again used to scatter in my room and changing clothes so that I could go out and play, and finally scattering my sportswear and putting on nightclothes.

So, on average, there were four makeovers per day.

And I never bothered to return them to their proper locations since I was too exhausted to pick them up.

Years passed, times changed, and I grew up, but my routines barely changed.

I began attending college, then taking professional course coaching, then heading to the institute and teaching, and eventually returning home (I decided to teach while I was still studying). Again, four makeovers.

You're probably wondering why I'm telling you this.

You've got to hang in there and let that sink in...

Additionally, I've always liked dressing up, so I had matching earrings, bag packs for each destination, and matching footwear.

By the end of the week, my room transformed into a market square. Everything was well out of order, so on weekends I would pick the four quadrants of the bedsheet, tie a fine knot, set it aside, spread a new bedsheet, and go about my business.

I only cleaned my room once a month when I saw four sheets stacked up in one corner with no one to scold me because I was always so preoccupied with something else that cleaning was never a priority.

But there's no disputing that my mind was constantly

racing, and peace was not a pleasant companion.

Things were going well for me, but I was not making any progress.

I was in decent shape, but I wasn't in decent health.

I was content, but not completely satisfied.

So, the clutter outside of me led to even more clutter inside of me.

Most of the time, I was unsure of what needed to be done.

The concentration was weak.

Distractions had taken control.

There was no direction in life.

The only explanation was bad room maintenance, which left me with no incentive to do better in life and made it difficult to find things in my room.

One wonderful day, I set myself the goal of keeping things in place for three days, then five, then seven, then fifteen, then a month, and finally forever.

The most significant change it made in my life was how it made room for more, both in my room and in my thoughts.

With a clean room, I discovered: (PEPCI)

- Positivity
- Energy
- Productivity
- Creativity
- Ideas for Relaxation

My grades began to improve and I became more contemplative and calmer, with more focus and concentration.

There was a sudden burst of energy in my body. My room and my life started to fall into harmony.
That's when I understood how cleaning improves one's life.

Here is a list of 15 challenges that you can take on each day to help you become more organized.

The 'DE-CLUTTER YOUR LIFE CHALLENGE' is what it's called.

Day 1- Get your closet in order.

Day 2 - Get your books organized.

Day 3 - Organize your bedroom.

Day 4 - Organize your side tables.

Day 5 - Sort through your mail.

Day 6 - Get your kitchen in order.

Day 7- Donate belongings that are no longer valuable to

you.

Day 8 - Make some room on your PC.

Day 9 - Wash your vehicles.

Day 10 - Clean out your refrigerator.

Day 11 - Go over old papers and messages.

Day 12 - Organize your shoe rack.

Day 13 – Empty your backpack and pack it.

Day 14 - Make very sure your desk is free of clutter.

Day 15 - Uninstall apps you don't use from your phone.

The following are some of the lesser-known perks of keeping your belongings in order:
    1. Best pass-time activity.
2. Soothing when accompanied by music.
3. A distraction from your distractions.
4. It keeps you occupied.
5. It reduces your screen time.
6. A lovely "Me-time" activity.

Have you ever tried to declutter your home yet struggled to discard the items?
If so, you are not alone.
    One fine day, my acquaintance approaches me and says, "The biggest obstacle I face is reducing the amount of stuff I own, to achieve simplicity and order in my life. However,

selecting which things to release is hindering my efforts. I always pick something up and think, "I will definitely need this later," which prevents me from discarding it.

I explained to her:

I recently underwent a significant decluttering at home.

I needed to get rid of a lot of items. Like you, I was reluctant to throw away a lot of items. A lone voice in my head kept telling me "You'll require this at some point. You must not throw it."

I had to quiet that voice. Here's what I found to be effective.

I started by establishing a straightforward rule.

First, whatever I hadn't utilized in the previous four months was immediately a candidate for destruction.

Second, I told myself that I could always get it back if I really wanted it after getting rid of it. I accepted the chance that I might have to purchase it again.

I felt so liberated after taking this action. I was able to let go of my worries about throwing away stuff I might—but probably—never need again.

Third, I resolved to discard two items every day.

Two seemed manageable because I could do it in a few minutes. As the weeks went by, I grew more at ease with getting rid of stuff. Action leads to more action. Two products per day eventually increased to three, four, then five, and so on.

My house was gradually becoming less and less cluttered. :)

You've probably seen that I'm a huge believer in making small, steady progress.

Try the technique I used if you want to get rid of things that are just taking up space.

It takes time, but it is effective!

Include this in your morning ritual. It won't seem like much of an effort because it only takes a few minutes. You'll be shocked by how much stuff you throw out over the next few weeks, eventually.

CHAPTER TWO

Be Productive

My go-to response when someone asks me what I'm doing is?

It reads, "I'm busy doing nothing."

Time flies by with practically everything still undone.

What am I doing?

- scrolling feed,
- searching for more relevant memes and quotes,
- mindlessly eating,
- snoozing to kill time,
- watching humorous and occasionally spooky videos, or
- The list continues forever.

I'm sure that the majority can relate to the fact that days go by without us accomplishing anything productive, but we still pretend to be busy with activities we haven't even begun. My friend, you are not alone if you could resonate with this.

After your cleaning and de-cluttering session; you will sense energies flowing inside of you. So, you need to utilize them wisely to increase your productivity.

You see, there is a difference between being productive and being busy.

Being productive means making the most of your time and not idly staring at the wall or scrolling through your feed.

Do you know what your problem is?

You are not tired.

You are not falling short of time.

You are only occupied with fleeting pleasures, fooling yourself into thinking you have endless time, but you are not wasting time. Years of your youth are being wasted by time.

Is it too late?

Maybe.

Can I still start?

Yes.

Will I make progress?

Depends on how genuinely I want it.

Why am I not productive?

Overly difficult work or boredom with tasks.

What do I do now?

Read carefully.

First things first.

I don't want you to switch on that ninja mode for a day and shirk things off for the rest of the month.

Instead, what I want you to do is take small steps CONSISTENTLY.

Do you get it?

Yes, consistency is the key to all the blocked opportunities in your life.

So, let us start from the start.

Day 1: Get up and sit in bed, refrain from lying down again and do some breathwork and stretch yourself.

Day 2: Get out and make your bed so that you don't feel tempted to go back again.

Day 3: Have a healthy breakfast, keep it slow, and don't rush-it'll keep you energized for the day.

Day 4: Organize your desk and write down the things that need immediate attention. Do it without thinking twice.

Day 5: Avoid spending your morning time on the phone. It's a mere distraction, if you wish to search for something while doing your work prefer using a PC/laptop which got no access to social media. Do not forget to turn off unnecessary notifications on the phone.

Day 6: Plan your day, a day before - you'll save time thinking and invest more time in doing it. Strike off the task you did alongside, it'll give you a push.

Day 7: We unwantedly spend a lot of time thinking about what to cook/eat. So, create a plan for a week and follow it without fail.

Day 8: Whenever you start to panic thinking that you are losing it or feeling anxious just go for a walk, it can be a quick one. Go get some fresh air and listen to music, if possible. This will help you get over your anxiety in no time and motivate you.

Day 9: No matter how busy you are, exercise for 30 minutes every day. You can wriggle, do yoga, hit the gym, or go for a brisk walk. You'll continue to be physically and mentally productive.

Day 10: Before going to sleep, read a few pages—preferably a chapter—of a book. Now, the focus of this book should revolve around whatever piques your curiosity. It might even be a brief tale with morals. The goal is to refrain from accessing social media right before sleeping.

Day 11: Avoid watching videos online to give yourself more personal time. If you chose not to use social media and instead buried yourself in a film. You failed.

Day 12: Write out your goals for your life and get to work on them. No one is interested in your wish list. You are compensated for carrying out your thoughts, not for thinking them out. You will differentiate yourself from others as an outcome of this.

Day 13: Take ten minutes to meditate. It's important to do it frequently because it recharges your body and soul. Avoid spending too much time worrying about your phone's dying batteries and neglecting to recharge your worn-out soul.

Day 14: Take a pause whenever necessary. Over rest is rust and under rest is depletion. Create a balance.

Day 15: Get enough sleep. We are going to discuss it at length in the next chapter and stay hydrated. Your body is nearly 70% water.

The following are some of the lesser-known perks of keeping yourself productive:

1. Lesser stress
2. Greater focus
3. Lesser procrastination
4. Greater time freedom
5. Lesser distractions
6. Greater energy

Have you ever begun working seriously only to get bored with it or wish to quit so you could spend the rest of your life doing nothing?

So, you're not by yourself.

One day, my neighbour comes to me and says she wants to quit her job because it is too stressful and had left her worried. She wants to spend her days relaxing instead. She lately even changed jobs, yet she was still in distress.

I told her that working hard is more important than lazing around. If you are exhausted, take some time off and go on vacation. You can always choose to fix difficulties rather than clipping them entirely.

Idleness is the root of all social ills; it makes you emotionally and physically ill, therefore just because you are struggling in your career doesn't mean you should quit trying.

You'll undoubtedly feel better after you learn to manage your time and career.

Thank me later.

CHAPTER THREE

Sleep Schedule and Night Routine

Fun fact: We all got exactly the same 24 hours to work on ourselves.

Some use them and make progress.

While others waste them and perish.

I'm not asking you to monitor every action you take, but I am trying to emphasize the importance of being aware of what you are doing.

Human resource is the most vital of all the resources since, without people, all other resources are futile.

You must therefore take care of yourself because you are PRECIOUS.

You will soon die if you don't put yourself first.

Many a time we end up saying:

I couldn't sleep well or
the beauty sleep wasn't sound enough or

it was a disrupted slumber or
I woke up in the middle of the night or
slept late and woke up early and all day long stayed
irritated.

Do you call it a life?

Do you call it taking rest?

Do you call it charging and restoring your batteries?
    Well, you are highly mistaken.

You must obtain appropriate rest and recovery time.

Additionally, we tend to overthink at night since, most of
the time, after finishing our work and tasks, we lay in bed,
desiring to fall asleep, but fail horribly, and begin to
overthink everything. We frequently revisit some
memories and consider the actions we could have taken
and the words we could have said. And this overthinking
isn't always about nice things.

We all give life to our fantasy world.

Yes, it all happens in the night-time.

Hours go by as you roll around in bed either overthinking
or watching videos, and now you're sleeping with the guilt
of not going to bed earlier and making a promise to go to
bed on time from tomorrow.

I hope I was able to make it clear where the crisis lies, now
let's speak about the solution.

Day 1: Regardless of how awful your day was, something positive must have happened. I urge you to write it down, either in a notebook or in the notes section of your phone, and not just to say it out loud. This will lift your spirits.

Day 2: Take a warm shower or a moisturizer to massage some pressure points, and your nerves will ease out and release tension.

Day 3: If you wish to make some real progress, avoid using your phone for at least an hour before bed because if you sit down intending to search for something, an hour will pass; if you read a good meme, 50 more will be read; if you push yourself to watch that one last video or episode, ten more will be watched. Therefore, stop the cycle for yourself and not for me.

Day 4: Drink a cup of warm water. This easy yet powerful technique will aid in digestion, induce sleep, and help you avoid the temptation of all forms of caffeine intake before bed.

Day 5: If you can't fall asleep right away, read for a while or listen to some soothing music instead of picking up the phone once more. Make a comfortable place to sleep.

Day 6: Pause for a moment.

Day 7: Light some fragrant candles or lamps.

Day 8: Stretch or practice yoga before going to bed.

Day 9: Be thankful. (We are going to talk about it shortly)

Day 10: Plan your tasks for the following day, your outfit for the day, your food, and so on.

Day 11: Pray and meditate.

Day 12: Organize your area. Your anxiety will decrease, and you won't be as tempted to use your phone.

Day 13: Prefer a light dinner. Don't go hungry to bed as well. You can have some cereal, fruit, or dry fruits.

Day 14: If necessary, set an alarm.

Day 15: Don't check your emails, news feeds, or texts right before dozing off to sleep.

The following are some of the lesser-known perks of fixing your sleep cycle:

1. Improve your mood.
2. Think more clearly.
3. Perform better in school or at work.
4. Think more clearly and get along better with people.
5. Get sick less frequently.
6. Maintain a healthy weight.
7. Lower your risk for serious health issues, like diabetes and heart disease.
8. Make wise decisions.
9. prevent accidents — for instance, drowsy drivers are responsible for thousands of car accidents.

I remember, once, half sleeping in the chair beside me was my colleague.

He is an ardent believer in sleeping for 4-5 hours and takes pleasure while explaining how it is enough, he thinks we are young and too much sleep isn't required. To which I responded, "very well said."

He survives on coffee dregs and refuses to sleep appropriately and leaves no stone unturned in exhausting himself yet standing upright every morning.

I became observant but never interjected.

I soon noticed him making careless errors, failing to pay attention to details, and starting to feel ill, for which he blamed the worsening pollution in Delhi. As a result, he became anxious and irritated.

If you too could resonate, read carefully.

Nobody actually knows how many hours of sleep are ideal.

Everything is dependent on how well you sleep and the quality of food you eat. To keep yourself upright, it is suggested that you should sleep for 7-8 hours each night.

<u>Your body will become ill and seek restitution if you don't give it the rest it requires</u>.

You can count on me for this one. :/

CHAPTER FOUR

Be Fit as a Fiddle

I am astounded by how quickly time is rushing while new technology has made our lives simpler, it has also worn down our patience. We expect practically everything to happen instantly, without any real effort on our part.

Hungry?... Ready to cook and eat preserved food.

Get fit?... Drive to the gym to walk on the treadmill and use the bicycle.

Eat healthily?... The pizza is topped with bell peppers and tomatoes.

Drink juice?... Cheers to sugary tetra-packed products.

Clean the house?... Buy vacuum cleaners and dishwashers.

Thank you for making my life easier and my health a matter of mockery.

People have the audacity to claim that they put in a full day's work while eating pasta with extra cheese and having maids at their beck and call.

Yes, they do mourn their weight gain.

Expecting a pat on the back despite all the effort they put in.

Of sure, I say.

You deserve to have reality slapped right in the face.

People have already endured too much and are now gobbling pills like candies.

Headache?... here's a pill.

Want toned muscles?... here's a pill.

Muscles cramps?... here's a pill.

Any slight inconvenience?... here's a pill.

Well, understand this;

A subscription fee for the gym is cheaper than medical bills.

You will never fix your anxiety and depression by taking pills.

You are a customer of the doctor, and he is delighted that you are ill and wishes to see you frequently in his clinic.

Don't be a miser while investing in yourself:

Quality clothes
Quality work-out
Quality books
Quality mentors
Quality diet
Cheap investments= cheap results.

I know you like lazing around, and I also know you want to beat your inner couch potato (No judgment, we all have one); consider this;

Exercising has health benefits.

Exercising 4-5 days a week has mental benefits.

Exercising 4-5 days a week without music in nature has spiritual benefits.

Being in shape makes life much more enjoyable.

Hold your horses because what I want to provide is something that will endure forever rather than just a quick boost. I know you are already too amped up right now.

Here's what you can start with: (This schedule might vary from individual to individual as per their strengths and preferences.)

Day 1: 30 sit-ups, 30 squats, 15 push-ups, 45 seconds of plank x 3

Day 2: 30 leg raises, 10 burpees, 30 jumping jacks, 30-sec wall sit x 3

Day 3: 30 lunges, 30 crunches, 15 push-ups, 1-minute of

plank x 3

Day 4: 30 mountain climbers, 30 crunches, 30 squats, 1-minute of wall sit x 3

Day 5: 30 sit-ups, 20 push-ups, 15 squat jumps, 1-minute jump rope x 3

Day 6: 50 jumping jacks, 45 crunches, 30 butt kicks, 2-minute jump rope x 3

Day 7: 40 squats, 30 crunches, 25 burpees, 10-minute brisk walk x 3

Day 8: 25 leg raises,25 push-ups, 40 crunches, 10- minute jog x 3

Day 9: 45 jumping jacks, 30 mountain climbers, 30 sit-ups, 30-second wall sit x 3

Day 10: 30 squats,30 butt kicks,30 crunches, 1-minute plank x 3

Day 11: 30 squats, 30 mountain climbers, 30 lunges, 30-second tree pose x 3

Day 12: 30 leg raises, 30 sit-ups, 30 twists, 15-minute brisk walk x 3

Day 13: 20 reverse crunches,20 standing pull crunches, 20 front jacks x 3

Day 14: 20 narrow squats, 20 normal squats, 20 jumping

jacks x 3

Day 15: 30 cross crunches, 20 side raise, 5-minute jog x 3

The following are some of the lesser-known perks of staying fit:

1. Boost your mood .
2. Decrease your future healthcare costs.
3. Give yourself more confidence.
4. Help you sleep better.
5. Improve your posture.
6. Improve your skin.
7. Reduce back pain.
8. Reduce stress.
9. Relieve PMS symptons.

You know, a close friend is biologically gifted to be thin; regardless of what or how much she consumes, she stays the same, never gaining or losing an ounce, (we all have that one friend) but she isn't happy about it.

I thus asked her, "what was bothering her by chance?"

She was in good physical shape but unhappy mentally.

What ties the two together?

You see, even though you are physically healthy.

Your thoughts may be elsewhere.

What seems to be in good condition on the outside may be

deteriorating on the inside.

Exercise, therefore, aids in both physical and emotional recovery.

• 24 •

Got anxiety issues?... go for a walk.

Lack of focus?... play a sport.

Feeling low?... dance on your favourite track.

CHAPTER FIVE

Boss up!

Now that you know how to keep your environment organized, increase your productivity, get a good night's sleep, and stay in shape.

The following pedestal, which you must now mount to rule this world, is here.

The fact is, your energy talks for you before you even say a word.

Everywhere you walk, people will notice your appearance and posture.

Whether you like it or not, others will evaluate you based on how you appear and conduct yourself.

Get in shape and dress properly.

Now, when I tell you to dress decently, I'm not demanding you to wear designer or pricey clothing.

A person wearing an XYZ brand might look like a clown if the attire doesn't align with the frame of a person.

Everything depends on the outfit you choose.

Apart from that, I don't want you to stuff your closet with clothes.

Start by having a respectable wardrobe.

Wash your clothing gently.

Dry them off.

Look after them.

Once they fade, toss them away.

Clean your shoes.

Slip on socks.

Correctly roll the sleeves.

Learn how color contrast functions.

Comb your hair.

Keep your fingernails neat and short.

Attend to the bodily odour (use alum).

Prepare yourself.

Life is too short to endure it goofing around.

Know the event.

Plan in advance.

Go prepared.

Don't merely dress like an employee who needs the job when you're working in a corporate.

Level up in accordance with what the senior figures are wearing.

Ensure that you are noticeable among the crowd for it ensures quick raises.

Here are some tips on how to present oneself well enough and look professional. People from all walks of life can adapt these and excel:

Day 1: Know your body type and dress in form-fitting, breathable clothing. Your clothes should neither be so loose that it keeps falling off the frame nor choke you, or rips off at the slightest movement of your body.

Day 2: Pick colour schemes that go well with the colour of your skin.

Day 3: Maintain simplicity.

Day 4: Revealing more skin won't make you look more attractive. Dress in a classy manner. You'll get the admiration and respect of others.

Day 5: Wear what you feel comfortable in and do so with style. That's the real game.

Day 6: Avoid mindlessly following trends because you risk becoming a fashion victim. Only a clown believes he is being appreciated and respected for being different when in fact he is being laughed at. (P.S. this isn't about clowns.)

Day 7: Maintain a healthy posture and stand up straight.

Day 8: Understand the occasion and prepare your attire in advance.

Day 9: Give every aspect of your personality a smile and a sense of piety.

Day 10: Don't be hesitant to give yourself a makeover.

Day 11: Find your signature smell.

Day 12: Take care of your bad breath.

Day 13: Apply moisturizer to your skin. Dry, flaky skin appears unhealthy and lifeless.

Day 14: Keep your hair neat and tidy.

Day 15: Say no to cracked heels and dirty nails.

The following are some of the lesser-known perks of dressing well:

1. It makes you noticeable, you already got an edge.
2. You feel confident.
3. You become more likable and presentable.
4. Your social game elevates.
5. You are perceived to be self-aware.
6. You attract more opportunities.

One fine day, I was instilling in my students the value of maintaining a good posture and dressing up well, emphasizing that they should begin practicing it at a tender age so that it gets imprinted in their personalities and that dressing nicely isn't just restricted to special occasions.

A bright student of mine remarked that although we may change our posture, attire, and even physical fitness, there isn't much we can do to change our appearances, such as our facial features or skin tone.

It's true.

One interesting fact about India is that people here find light skin to be attractive and appealing. Yes, that's strange, but that's just how it is.

Another school of thought, however, argues that having clear, healthy skin is more important than having a fair complexion. Additionally, to do that, you only need sunlight, exercise, water, and a healthy diet—not those essential oils that con you and burn a hole in your pocket.

And when I talk about improving your appearance, I do not in any way advocate changing your features or going under the knife.

Let's say, a person is 4/10 in looks.

She/he can achieve a 6/10 by dressing appropriately and walking with grace and having pleasing manners.

She/he can improve to an 8/10 by becoming skilled, knowledgeable, and communicative.

She/he can achieve a score of 10/10 by becoming wealthy and one-of-a-kind.

You can see how by improving yourself, you can go from being a 4 to a 10.

Additionally, 90% of individuals aren't actually ugly; they're just too lazy to take a bath, maintain themselves, or dress nicely because those things require effort.

CHAPTER SIX

Step Out of your Safety Zone

As the saying goes, a rolling stone doesn't gather moss.

You never get out of date if you keep growing and are open to learning because you have mastered keeping up with change.

Most of the time, we believe that just because we have climbed a mountain and arrived at the summit in our respective fields, we are supreme yet learning is never over.

You must have encountered intellectuals who once shone but have now faded because they refuse to move forward with the times and adhere to outdated trends and approaches.

The trick is to avoid becoming too accustomed to what you are doing since that will mean the challenge is ended. Never stop pushing yourself to aim higher.

The cost of the new you is the old you.

Grow new skin every six months.

Transform yourself.

Monotony dulls the mind.

You may completely transform yourself in both positive and negative ways in a year. You can either get into a downward spiral with just one poor choice or level up with deliberate and thoughtful choices.

Nobody truly cares about timid introverts in the twenty-first century, so arm yourself with social skills. The challenge is that individuals are both ambitious and lazy. They desire the results but are unconcerned about putting in the necessary effort.

Here is how to get out of your comfy zone:

Day 1: Be able to initiate and carry on a conversation with a stranger.

Day 2: Don't wear anything similar to what you normally wear.

Day 3: Express gratitude to someone and then provide a reason.

Day 4: Try a new cooking recipe.

Day 5: Try a different exercise (aerobics, yoga, running, martial arts, and so on)

Day 6: Rekindle previous friendships and connections.

Day 7: Explore a new place by yourself in your town.

Day 8: Divert from your usual path to your destinations.

Day 9: Discuss with your friend a topic you have been avoiding.

Day 10: Learn a new skill.

Day 11: Try social media detox.

Day 12: Try a new cuisine/dish when dining out.

Day 13: Help somebody without them asking you but not forcefully.

Day 14: Surprise somebody with an act of kindness or a gift.

Day 15: Go on a day out all by yourself.

There is a plethora of other ways you might try to step outside your comfort zone. I gave you some, but you can also imagine some and email them to me at divya2jain1103@gmail.com

(Stepping outside of your safety zone includes things like this, too) :)

Some of the less well-known perks of pushing outside your safe zone include the following:

1. An instant confidence boost.
2. Making your hidden talents known.

3. Using your energies as a channel.
4. Increase your productivity and creativity.
5. Gaining new experiences helps you mature.
6. Develop intelligence and common sense.
7. Set your phone aside.
8. Leave your thoughts alone.
9. Become less self-conscious in social situations and interactions.

Additionally, if you feel:

The world is evolving but still, your personal growth and learning have come to a standstill.

Well, needless to say, you have developed this victim mentality and comforting yourself with soothing lies.

Don't you think you are the barricade in your progress?

Because let's be honest, if you were determined enough and not feeding your mind with a handful of justifications and excuses then you would have been in a better place by now.

I'm neither a mind reader nor have I met you yet I can tell with dire conviction that;

You are aware that you are stuck, though.

You are aware that you desire to advance.

You are aware that you must establish yourself.

You are aware of your greater value.

You are confident in your abilities.

You are aware of your potential.

You are aware of how you can alter your life forever.

And yet, you are unwilling to take action.

Why?

Still not ready, are you?

Are you awaiting the ideal moment?

You're awaiting some spare time, right?

Do you plan to begin it on Monday, the following week, the following month, the following year, or just forever?

Set a rule.

Just give yourself five minutes to do whatever you want to do.

Just five minutes.

You'll likely keep doing it.

The difficult part is commencing a task.

Things get simpler once you have it in your grip.

Next, begin by taking small steps.

Solving one puzzle,

Performing one push-up,

Performing one asana,

Writing one page,

Drinking one glass of water,

Paying one debt,

Sending one piece of mail,

Making one phone call,

Walking one lap,

Closing one deal.

Then, repeat it.

The trick is to keep it simple at first and avoid complexity.

Now, I sincerely apologize to everyone who hopes to succeed instantly.

This is not taking place.

Be focused on your task at hand.

Do not be concerned that everything revolves around you.

Time will pass you by.

The accomplishment is easier, the simpler the procedure.

So, please stop blocking your blessings.

Here are a few habits you have to leave behind so that you can get access to a *savage version* of yourself.

1. *Need to be liked and appreciated* –

Break away from the confines of being acceptable. Whatever you accomplish, there will always be people who do not appreciate you.

And it's not your responsibility to make people like you. There is no need for outside validation to make you believe in yourself.

Because ***"If you don't believe in yourself, who will?"***

2. *Need to control everything* –

I realize that you want to take complete responsibility for the task at hand, but resist the temptation to be in charge every time.

There are a couple of issues over which we have no control, so relax.

3. *Need to maintain toxic relations*-

Regardless of what history you share with a person; if they're toxic and are not contributing to your growth. LEAVE.

It's hard to achieve anything amidst chaos and negativity.

4. *Need to be perfect*-

Oh, my dear! Perfectionism exerts force and triggers the desire to be flawless. You are already amazing.

5. *Need to get overnight success*-

In this day and age, everything happens in the blink of an eye. Success and empires do not emerge overnight. So, let go of your desire to become an overnight sensation.

Remember that 'Rome was not constructed in a day, but the bricks were laid every hour.'

Success is a fine blend of consistency and hard work.

CHAPTER SEVEN

Express Gratitude and Journaling

Wants are recurring in nature.

As soon as one want is satisfied, another one replaces it.

Something you desired at some point in time and got by putting in the effort.

Now, you hardly care about it.

Come 'on that was something you strived for.

Now that you have it, you take it for granted and think if you can have it, anybody can have it.

We do a lot to attain something yet what do we do to retain it?

Little or nothing.

Well, yes.

Yes, I'm talking to you about you.

And you know what exactly happens when you take things for granted?

You lose it. You lose it forever, and even if you have it, it isn't the same as before.

That's fair enough.

Alongside, precisely at that moment gratitude emerges.

Gratitude expression helps you stay rooted and grounded.

How frequently do you express gratitude for the many resources you take from mother Earth?

Interesting.

While chasing your desires, it is never too late to begin appreciating what you already have.

What you should do and be grateful for are as follows:

Day 1: The best thing that happened to you today?

Day 2: What makes you happy and why?

Day 3: Someone who helped you and how?

Day 4: An unexpected act of kindness from someone.

Day 5: A possession you are thankful for.

Day 6: Who made you smile at your lowest?

Day 7: A lovely sight you encountered today.

Day 8: The best creation of nature?

Day 9: A challenge or phobia you overcame?

Day 10: An element you appreciate about your house.

Day 11: Take a photo of the section of this book that you enjoyed the most, or give your valuable feedback or express gratitude on Instagram and DM/tag me @divya jain1103 and get featured on my profile.

Day 12: Supportive figures in your life who encouraged you to advance.

Day 13: What talent do you have?

Day 14: How you extended assistance to a person who couldn't reciprocate.

Day 15: A moment you were pleased with yourself.

Day 16: What gives you a sense of privilege?

Day 17: An energizing experience.

Day 18: A sumptuous meal.

Day 19: A source of peace for you.

Day 20: A distinctive quality you admire about yourself.

Day 21: A person whose presence improved your life.

Did you notice that I created a 15-day schedule for every chapter before this one, but this chapter is 21 days long?

Oh, yes.

Little extra works wonder.

Be grateful for it just like I'm to be able to help you. :)

Did you just smile?

Wow.
I still have something to say to you.
Writing in a journal is an art form that can help you overcome self-doubt and reduce overthinking.

You will learn to live in the present rather than the past or the future as a result of this exercise.
How is it different from expressing gratitude?

It brings clarity.

Sometimes, all you need to do is clear your head by doing some conscious self-talk.

You can't always feel at ease disclosing all that goes through your mind. Therefore, journaling clears the mental haze.

Let's start now: Put it down on paper in your handwriting.

Day 1: What can I do to improve my physical health?

Day 2: How can I adopt the qualities I most respect in others?

Day 3: What should I simply stop doing?

Day 4: What are the three areas of my life that I'd like to improve?

Day 5: What do I need to let go of?

Day 6: My short-term goals.

Day 7: My long-term goals.

Day 8 AM I settling for less than what I deserve?

Day 9: What have I learned from my previous errors?

Day 10: What is the right approach to sum up my work ethic?

Day 11: What am I doing with my spare time?

Day 12: Do I use the internet to help my own development? What steps should I take, if not?

Day 13: How do I manage my feelings?

Day 14: How can I look after myself?

Day 15: How can I better handle my finances?

Day 16: How can I start giving my mental health more priority?

Day 17 AM I satisfied with the direction my life is taking?

Day 18: How do I judge myself from within?

Day 19: What talent would I teach others if I could?

Day 20: How can my experiences help me grow?

Day 21: What do I feel like when I'm all by myself?

You should reflect on these issues and stir your mind to better yourself and your life.

The following are a few benefits of expressing gratitude and journaling that are less generally known:

1. It makes you less anxious.
2. Minimizes aggression.
3. You can sleep soundly.
4. It strengthens you.
5. Your outlook is more optimistic.
6. You're more sympathetic and caring.
7. It improves your sense of self.
8. Your relationships are stronger.
9. Your physical health is enhanced.

Once, I was out with a friend, and we were sitting in a café sipping our coffee, and she was casually looking around and exclaimed, "how happy everyone else was around us" and how she had lately felt incomplete.

Which prompted me to ask, "Do you know them?"

She declined.

I asked if you had any idea what they had gone through or were going through.

She declined.

So, who are you and I to say whether their lives are perfect and ours isn't?

Dear, you tend to forget your blessings when you see how fortunate the other person is. That very instant prompts you to express gratitude and wish well for others.

We ought to be able to see through as well as observe what this world is presenting to us.

We all have our own emotional baggage as well as our own blessings.

And if you feel unsatisfied, incomplete, and inept, try visiting an orphanage or an old age home.

Life is too short to live ungratefully.

CHAPTER EIGHT

Achieving Mental Well-being and Inner Calm

Well,

Have you ever thought about the ultimate goal of your life?

Is it to get into your dream college?

Is it to get a degree?

Is it to buy the best house?

Is it to go on a world tour?

Is it to buy a sports car?

Is it to get featured in an esteemed column of a magazine?

Is it to be able to buy anything and everything?

Is it to get a Government Job?

Is it to get fame?
   Is it to get power and respect?

And the list goes on and on...

What do you believe is the one thing that we are all running for?

If it's anything from the list above, my friend, you'll be hungry for the rest of your life because an individual's 'wants' are never-ending and repeating in nature as already explained in the previous chapter.
This era has taught us to strive for more while losing ourselves in the process. We live in a world filled with wishful thinking. The physical and rational being desires more of everything.

But WAIT!

Is it going to make you happy?

Temporarily? ... Yes.

Permanently?... No.

Why?

Because the ultimate goal of life is to have "peace of mind."

And I can't stress it enough, but sooner or later you'll get to a point in life when all you'll crave is "Peace of Mind."

Allow me to simplify it for you...

You can have the best job yet feel terrible inside,

You can have the best house yet feel lonely,

You can have all the money yet feel barren.

Long Story Short: If it doesn't give you peace of mind, it's too expensive and is just not worth your while.

So, it's high time that you outgrow things that no longer help you evolve or give you inner peace.

Reminder: Your relationships shouldn't be a battlefield for you!

Swiftly moving ahead,
You've gone a long way, and I applaud you for your accomplishments. The prime issues have been addressed, however, there is more room to improve.

Do you know whom you spend most of your time with?

Your family?... Nay.

Your friends?... Nay.

Your pet? ... Nay.

Your colleagues? ... Nay.

Yourself?... Yeah.

You've probably heard of people developing relationships with others who make their lives happier and more productive and refuse to stand with those who are destructive and nasty.

But if you are toxic to yourself, what can be done?

When you're not at peace, what can be done?

If you're having trouble focusing or falling asleep, what can be done?

If your own company feels hateful, what can be done?

If you're overthinking and just won't stop, what can be done?

I recall reading George Herbert's poem "The Pulley," which follows the premise that when God created mankind, he had a cup of blessings in hand and thought to himself, "Why don't I give some of it to mankind? I'll compress all of the wealth in the world into a self-sufficient human life."

First, he gave people strength, which made a route for the rest of the qualities. Then he poured out beauty; then, wisdom; then, lofty morals; and delight; but after he'd almost finished emptying the cup of the blessing, God held back, knowing that only peace was left in the bottom.

He stated: "People would be so peacefully pleased with their lives on earth that they wouldn't think to adore the

God who created all this goodness if I also offered this last wonderful gift to my creation. They would love the things I gave them and forget all about me. If it happened, I would lose something, and so would the humans!

So, he decided that humans will be richly gifted but also worn out by the test of time, and by a nagging want to return home to me and arranged things this way: Humans can keep all the other benefits I've given them, but they'll also have a continual, regretful, distracting yearning.

All in all, everyone is lacking in peace of mind, but there is a never-ending quest to get it.

Here is what you can do to attain peace of mind:

Day 1: Worship God, keep it simple. You can either go to a temple or in the lap of nature, God is found everywhere. Express yourself fully. He hears you. He can see right through you, so don't bother about your word choice. Seek the divine. Additionally, you can assist those in need who cannot reciprocate by giving you anything. Seek forgiveness for the sins you have committed. Believe in God because he is all-mighty.

Day 2: If your day was stressful, take a minute to unwind your body. Engage in deep breathing, and use a massage with soothing oil to assist your body to relax.

Day 3: Give someone a firm hug while you both take five deep breaths. It'll keep you rooted.

Day 4: Prepare a cup of tea or coffee for yourself and focus entirely on it. Take your chance to enjoy the flavour.

Day 5: Try walking outdoors. Look around you, take in the greenery and tranquillity.

Day 6: Pay attention to your thoughts and your mental activity. Be kind to yourself.

Day 7: Smile in the mirror because you are a wonderful creation of God with a universe within you.

Day 8: Consume food and pay attention to your five senses—taste, smell, sight, touch, and sense—in aggregate. Just do it.

Day 9: Try aromatherapy. We feel better when we can breathe pleasant things.

Day 10: Examine your body and pay attention to any physical feelings. Release negative emotions as you exhale. Take a moment to savor pleasant feelings and inhale them in.

Day 11: Take a meditative bath. Turn the lights out and take a break. Concentrate on the warmth and sensations you experience as the water flows over your body.

Day 12: Immediately leave the environment that provides you with uneasiness.

Day 13: Call a loved one you haven't spoken to for a long time.

Day 14: Sing along while you listen to your favorite music.

Day 15: Read a fresh book.

You are going to see a sea difference having practiced these.

Here comes the perks for keeping your mind calm and peaceful:
1. Encourages a healthy lifestyle
2. Provides mental clarity.
3. Increases energy.
4. Increases self-awareness.
5. Reduces pain and tension.
6. Makes you happier.
7. Slows aging.
8. Helps you sleep well.
9. Helps with weight loss.

Many times when we find ourselves in a position, we are powerless to escape it; it affects us even when we don't want it to, and it eventually consumes us from the inside out. These are the circumstances that are out of our control; even if we wanted to, we really can't make them right. It disturbs our serenity and leaves us numb.

What are these circumstances?
• family problems
  • unexpected death of a loved one.
  • unhealthy parents.
  • loving a person who doesn't love you back.

Some issues cannot be resolved. Life is unfair.

What is the best course of action?

God offers you strength and shade at this point. All you need to do is surrender.

A person who communicates with God will arrive at every destination.

A true and heartfelt prayer transforms the pray-er.

Additionally, "DO NOT FORGET TO FORGET"

Now, that's something you need to understand, your mind is a powerful-powerful weapon that can either work for you or against you.

We tend to recall the incidents that traumatized, frightened, and afflicted us in the past.

As a result, we become too afraid to expose our vulnerabilities and question everything that life brings forth.

Lil confused?

Let me simplify it for you,

When someone makes an extra effort to assist you.

Do you wonder, "What's their hidden purpose? "

When someone shows you that they love you.

Do you wonder, "Are they genuinely serious about It?"

When someone doesn't respond appropriately.

Do you wonder "where you went wrong?"

If the answer to any of these questions was 'YES.' Then continue reading.

Let me give you a little explanation of how the brain works. Our brain continuously picks up on danger signals or negative energy from our environment to prepare us ready for them; it essentially builds a defense mechanism.

For instance, when we were young, our family or friends mistreatment of us made a lasting, terrible effect on our brains.

Our brain processed this as an input (a bad vibe), and as an output, it prepared a defense mechanism: "If anyone uses the same tactic to trigger us in the future, either we will feel terrible about it and cry and yell or we will start accepting it as truth and over-think about it leaving us to question our self-worth."
What causes this to occur?

Because YOU aren't willing to let go of the sorrow, your memory store keeps refreshing the memories and smacking them in your face repeatedly to make sure you never forget what happened to you.
We must therefore let go of past suffering, create new memories, and approach life with a fresh perspective if we want to manifest better and attract riches.

Trust me;

DON'T FORGET TO FORGET:

The old pain,
The childhood bullying,
The complaints our parents and teachers had,
The past failures,
The feeling of being isolated,
The failed relationships,
The low scores,
The lost match,
The weight issue,

Because it is preventing you from experiencing the opportunity, love, and joyful life that are going to come into your life. As a lesson, you don't have to always carry around the weight of helplessness and sorrow.
Here are some techniques you can use to cope with it and overcome the filth that has been keeping you from having healthy experiences and is rotting inside your mind:

<u>1. Acceptance</u>

You can find the strength to let go and make room for new experiences by accepting what happened to you in the past, especially in light of how terrible it was. Until we stop defending why something bad happened to us, whether or not it was justified?

It will be a conversation with no clear conclusion. Therefore, just accept it and tell yourself, "YES, it happened, and I can't change it, but I can choose to move on.

Additionally, if something from your past is bugging you, resist the urge to divert your attention or keep yourself occupied to escape what is inside of you and eating you away. Instead, have a conversation with yourself, ask the important questions, and confront the potentially catastrophic situation. I strongly believe that you already possess the answers.

2. Express Gratitude

Be grateful for both the good and terrible moments since they shaped you and provided you with life experience and wisdom. Be grateful for all the hardships life has given you since each stage of life will require a new version of you.

3. Welcome new experiences with open arms

Well, needless to say, but;

Your new friends are probably not going to bully you the way the old ones did.

Your new boss is probably not going to piss you off the way the old one did.

Your new teacher is probably not going to discourage you the way the old one did.

Your new lover is probably not going to disappoint you or cheat on you the way the old one did.

Your "New Self" is not going to question its existence and self-worth the way the "Old You" did.

Don't worry, don't stress it out too much. The universe is working out for you, my friend.

4. Don't forget the lesson

Life gives each one of us a unique battle to fight,

Every pain was given to you; to make you strong,

Every failure was given to you; to make you more grounded.

Every hardship was given to you; to make you mature.

Don't let it go to waste and become a victim of more struggles and hardships in the future.

Keep in mind what you learned from it to avoid being a slave of a similar situation in the future. Life is too precious to waste time dwelling on the same errors and blunders.

5. Set firm Boundaries

Boundaries act as a guard for you, preventing you from going through the same terrible experiences you have had in the past with various groups of individuals. Because life is trying to see if you are still the same ignorant person you were before, don't compromise on them, and won't entertain anyone who doesn't respect them enough.

CHAPTER NINE

Junk the Junk

There should be no compromise at all when it comes to what you put in your mouth and mind.

The saying "A healthy mind dwells in a healthy body" is wise advice.

The most charming fashion statement is a fit, healthy body.

You can't expect your mind to function efficiently if you just devour stale, fried, processed food that has been preserved.

Negative influences have the benefit that it is simple to adjust to them.

Will you eat a pizza, if I ask you to? You won't hesitate.

Would you eat a truffle cake if I asked you to? You will adore it.

Will you eat some fries if I ask you to? You won't oppose the offer.

Of course.

Who would act that way?

We are aware that these foods have poor nutritional value but are dopamine-stimulating. When you consume something delicious, your brain releases this hormone. It drives you crazy.

Your laziness is another factor contributing to your preference for junk food.

Eating healthily is a conscious decision.

A healthy lifestyle requires effort.

It takes effort to be able to withstand something for momentary pleasure.

It requires work to maintain discipline.

And masses are mere slaves to their temptations and worship yolo psyche.

Trust me, the doctors of the future will prescribe fasting for almost everything.

There is no denying the fact that we are fully conscious fast food is bad for us, it is called junk food for a reason, additionally, even when we decide to eat healthily those around us aren't always very supportive of this fact and encourage us to just taste it once or insist on taking a small bite. If you admit it, this is a negative sum game because,

1. You broke your own discipline.

2. You weren't particularly pushed by goals. A person who has attained clarity about what they should and shouldn't eat remains unaffected and dismisses those who try to entice them.

3. You are easy to persuade because of your loose frame.

4. A quick wave of remorse and guilt follows.

5. A pledge is taken, then broken again.

However, these individuals are frequently observed on any occasion that serves them such delights with their plates piled high, bragging about how careful they are with their nutrition. What a paradox!

Many even give lectures on how to maintain balance. For instance, if you ate a burger, you would go to the gym and work out. But where would the energy come from?

I see!

Going to the gym is not a big deal; the challenge is not giving in to your cravings for mindless eating.

Outside of the gym is where the true test of weight loss is administered.

Now that you are aware of what I'm referring to, you are looking for solutions.

Day 1: Increasing the number of vegetables you eat.

Day 2: Limit your consumption of refined sugar to only fruits and jaggery.

Day 3: Swap out the deep-fried chips for some nuts.

Day 4: Eat some dates or fruit instead of toffees or cookies.

Day 5: Skip dairy products for a day and compare the results.

Day 6: Skip the meat today and lead a vegetarian lifestyle.

Day 7: Include green vegetables in your diet.

Day 8: Set aside a day for exclusively fresh fruit and drinks. You'll experience energy.

Day 9: Avoid fast food, prepare a tasty, nutritious meal for yourself, and try substituting unhealthy items. Consider using semolina (suji) for white flour or milk or sweet chocolate for dark chocolate.

Day 10: Consume 10 glasses of water so that you are constantly peeing and have no time for mourning or feeling overwhelmed.

Day 11: No alcohol or cigarettes.

Day 12: No caffeine.

Day 13: No processed food.

Day 14: Keep your dinner light.

Day 15: No white bread.

Defy your temptations and resist them. The only residence your soul has is your physical being.

Make sure everything is cleansed lest the soul shall flee and you perish.

Some lesser-known perks of eating right;

1. Helps lose weight
2. Improves heart health
3. Increases immunity
4. Boosts brain health
5. Improves digestion
6. Strengthens bones
7. Delays aging
8. Improves skin health
9. Reduces stress
10. You start to look better and feel better.

With the rising cases of obesity among youth and the "size doesn't matter" or "accept me the way I am" psyche.

We're not getting too far.

Before we even attempt to start a revolution, we must correct our ideologies.

Being overweight not only lowers your self-esteem but also brings on a host of health issues down the road.

With this, I wish you all the best in life.

9 7798888 92 30403